SPOTLIGHT ON NATURE
MOOSE

LISA M. BOLT SIMONS

CREATIVE EDUCATION · CREATIVE PAPERBACKS

Published by Creative Education and Creative Paperbacks
P.O. Box 227, Mankato, Minnesota 56002
Creative Education and Creative Paperbacks are imprints
of The Creative Company
www.thecreativecompany.us

Design and production by Blue Design, Inc.
Art direction by Graham Morgan

Images by Dreamstime/Karayuschij, 3, 29; Getty Images/Chase Dekker Wild-Life Images, 14, 17, imageBROKER/Thomas Sbampato, 4–5, Manuel ROMARIS, 12, Scott Suriano, 27, Tom Walker, 23; Pexels/Chris F, 6, 16, 29, Dallin P, 29, Jay Cathcart, 28, Tomáš Malík, 21; Shutterstock/Imfoto, 10; Unsplash/Cora Leach, 15, Judy Beth Morris, 21, Luke Richardson, 24, Melina Kiefer, 11, Richard Lee, cover, 1, 9, Shivam Kumar, 18; Wikimedia Commons/Internet Archive Book Images, 8, 10, 14, 16, 20, 22, NPS Photo, 29

Every effort has been made to contact copyright holders for material reproduced in this book. Any omissions will be rectified in subsequent printings if notice is given to the publisher.

Copyright © 2026 Creative Education, Creative Paperbacks
International copyright reserved in all countries. No part of this book may be reproduced in any form without written permission from the publisher.

Library of Congress Cataloging-in-Publication Data
Names: Simons, Lisa M. Bolt, 1969- author
Title: Moose / by: Lisa M. Bolt Simons.
Description: Mankato, Minnesota : Creative Education and Creative Paperbacks, [2026] | Series: Spotlight on nature | Includes bibliographical references and index. | Audience: Ages 10-13 | Audience: Grades 4-6 | Summary: "An immersive wildlife book for upper-elementry and middle-school readers, featuring a captivating moose family narrative, stunning photography, and educational tools like infographics, a glossary, and an index. Explores species, habitats, and conservation, making it perfect for nature lovers and young conservationists"— Provided by publisher.
Identifiers: LCCN 2025017581 (print) | LCCN 2025017582 (ebook) | ISBN 9798895810781 library binding | ISBN 9798896800316 paperback | ISBN 9798895812044 ebook
Subjects: LCSH: Moose—Juvenile literature
Classification: LCC QL737.U55 .S556 2026 (print) | LCC QL737.U55 (ebook) | DDC 599.65/7—dc23/eng/20250730
LC record available at https://lccn.loc.gov/2025017581
LC ebook record available at https://lccn.loc.gov/2025017582

Printed in the United States

CONTENTS

MEET THE FAMILY   4
Moose of Denali National Park & Preserve

LIFE BEGINS   7
FEATURED FAMILY
Welcome to the World   8
First Meal   10

EARLY ADVENTURES   13
FEATURED FAMILY
Feeding Near the Forest   14
Give It a Try   16

LIFE LESSONS   19
FEATURED FAMILY
This Is How It's Done   20
Practice Makes Perfect   22

MOOSE CONSERVATION   25

Family Album Snapshots   28
Words to Know   30
Learn More   31
Index   32

MEET THE FAMILY

Moose of Denali National Park & Preserve

Denali National Park & Preserve in Alaska is four hours north of Anchorage, the state's capital. The huge park is six million acres (2,400,000 hectares). It only has one road. North America's tallest mountain, Denali, formerly known as Mount McKinley, rises to 20,210 feet (6,160 meters).

Founded in 1917, this diverse park has glaciers, inactive volcanoes, mountains, lakes, rivers, and forests. The **ecosystems** provide homes to more than 160 species of birds, including golden eagles, surfbirds, and black-billed magpies. No reptiles survive the cold here, but the amphibian wood frog lives in Denali's wetlands and forests. The majority of Denali's residents are invertebrates, like bumble bees and butterflies. The Big Five mammals—caribou, Dall sheep, wolves, grizzly bears, and moose—delight park visitors.

It's mid-May. A female moose, or cow, finds a dense area within some shrubs in an aspen forest inside the park. She finds a site that will protect her offspring and provide food. She mated about eight months ago. She stands rigid, her body contracting, ready to give birth.

CLOSE-UP
Hair

Baby moose are born with red-brown fur. As the baby grows, the fur turns to a light rust. Each hollow hair traps air inside, which provides insulation for the moose during the coldest months.

CHAPTER ONE
LIFE BEGINS

Moose are easy mammals to recognize, since they are the largest relative in the deer family. The largest moose live in Alaska and eastern Siberia, Russia. The males, or bulls, can weigh up to 1,600 pounds (725.7 kg). At the shoulder their height is about 6 feet tall (1.8 meters). The smallest moose live in southern Wyoming and in northeastern China. These bulls weigh up to 770 pounds (349.2 kg). Although smaller, female moose in Alaska can weigh up to 1300 pounds.

Antlers are the most distinguishing feature on a moose. They have a flat area with **tines** that point up. They are called "palmated" antlers because they look like a human palms turned up. Antlers grow every summer after a male turns one. They can reach 6 ft (1.8in) across, which is the height of the average adult male in the U.S.! Fully grown antlers weigh up to 60 pounds (27.2kg) or more. Moose fur ranges from golden or dark brown to

MOOSE MILESTONES

DAY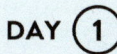

- Averages 30 pounds at birth
- Eats leafy plants
- Drinks mother's milk

almost black. Moose have bad eyesight, but they have an excellent sense of smell with their large **muzzle** and a sharp sense of hearing with their big ears. A large shoulder hump sits behind their head. A flap of skin called a dewlap or bell dangles from their throat.

Four subspecies of moose live in North America. The Alaskan moose live in Alaska and northwestern Canada. The Shiras moose live in the Rocky Mountains. The eastern moose live in eastern Canada and the northeastern United States. The northwestern moose lives in central Canada and North Dakota, Minnesota, and northern Michigan. Moose usually live in forested areas with a water source, such as a pond or stream.

Moose usually live alone. Females are alone or with their offspring. But during the breeding season, moose will form small groups. During

CLOSE-UP
Legs

Calves are born with legs strong enough to walk within hours after birth. As adults, moose use their legs to walk, trot 20 miles (32.2 km) per hour, run 35 miles (56.3 km) per hour, swim, and kick predators.

——— FEATURED FAMILY ———

Welcome to the World

The cow is finally ready to give birth. She kneels on her front legs, then folds her back legs until she's on the leafy ground. She's panting. Her body jerks, then lies still. She continues to pant. The cow's body jerks again, and a moose calf slips out of her mother. She reaches around and licks her slick newborn, a female. The newborn shakes her head, taking her first breaths. With shaky legs, the newborn eventually stands, falls, and stands again. As she adjusts to her new world on wobbly legs, her mother's body jerks again. The newborn's twin is born.

this time, the males, or bulls, can be dangerous or aggressive. Despite this, moose are not territorial.

Wolves and bears are natural predators for the moose, but healthy adults are rarely taken down. It's the much smaller calves that fall prey to hungry predators. Their mothers protect their offspring as much as they can as the calves fight to survive their first year.

① WEEK
- Can walk and swim
- Can outrun a human

② WEEKS
- Starts tasting other food

CLOSE-UP
Hooves

Hooves support the animal's large bodies by acting like snowshoes in the winter and boots on muddy ground. Moose also use their hooves like shovels to find food in the winter.

— FEATURED FAMILY —

First Meal

The mother licks the twin sister as the first newborn gathers her senses. She totters nearby, looking from mother to sister to shrubs, taking in her new world. Her tummy starts to rumble. She stumbles to her mother and tries to find her mother's teats to nurse. But they're on her mother's belly by her hind legs. The cow is still turned back, licking the second twin. After some time, the mother finally stands. Both newborns find the mother's teats to taste their first warm milk.

Moose comes from the Native Algonquin word **"MOOSH"** meaning "stripper and eater of bark."

5 MONTHS

- Grows to 10 times birth weight
- Sheds newborn coat for adult coat
- Weaned from mother's milk

LIFE BEGINS

CLOSE-UP
Muzzle

The moose uses its muzzle as an underwater eating tool, staying submerged for 50 seconds while its nostrils shut to keep water out.

CHAPTER TWO
EARLY ADVENTURES

Moose offspring are nowhere near the size of their tall mother. She is their fierce protector as the they wander through their habitat. She must fend off hungry bears with her kicks or lead her offspring into ponds or other water to avoid them in the summer. Protecting twins or triplets is even harder. Only one or two calves per ten cows survive to see the next spring. The male moose are nowhere in sight. They spend the summer alone, continuing to grow their massive antlers for mating season.

Calves begin to eat plants and twigs a couple of weeks after birth. When they come across ponds and streams, they put their muzzles into the water for pond lilies, weeds, and other **aquatic** vegetation. The calves continue to nurse. With all of this eating, the calves grow fast. By the time they are five months old, they weigh ten times their birth weight or close to 300 pounds (136.1 kg). By the time they're adults, they'll be eating between 40 and 60 pounds (18.1–27.2 kg) of food a day.

1 YEAR

- Chased off by mother before she gives birth again
- Males have started growing first set of antlers

CLOSE-UP
Communication

Bull moose make roar-bellows, croaks, and barks. Cows make moans and moo-bawl sounds. Cows also use a "distance-reducing" call to attract males.

— FEATURED FAMILY —

Feeding Near the Forest

The twins are a couple of weeks old. They wake in the middle of the shrubs, and the mother licks her twins. They rise and follow their mother. The family ventures out not far away to a patch of horsetails. The mother spreads her front legs to lean over and grab the stems with thin, narrow leaves with her lips. One twin, then the other, kneel to try this new food. They chew, swallow, regurgitate, and chew the horsetail stems more. Eventually, they swallow this new food. The twins nurse as their mother continues to eat.

Moose are plant-eaters, or herbivores. They eat a variety of plants, depending on where they live. Moose that live in the northernmost areas like Canada eat **deciduous** plants and twigs. But in Scandinavian countries in Europe, moose eat more conifers and mountain cranberries. In British Columbia, moose dine on highbush cranberries and firs. In North Dakota, moose eat crops like corn and soybeans and plants like sunflowers.

Moose are ruminants. Ruminants are hoofed animals with a special digestive system that better uses the plants they eat. Moose chew their food, digest it, **regurgitate** it, chew on the cud, or the food that comes back up, and swallow it again to be digested a second time. They chew thousands of times a day. They can even spend eight hours a day chewing their cud.

In the winter the predatory bears hibernate. The baby moose, although bigger and stronger, still need help from their tall mothers that that can plow through deep snow and offer protection from wolves. A mother's mighty kick can kill a wolf. If the mother and her offspring survive the winter, the adolescent moose is about to experience a huge change in its next stage of life.

(16) MONTHS

- Females reach reproductive maturity
- Males reach reproductive maturity

EARLY ADVENTURES

CLOSE-UP
Dewlap

Both mature male and female moose have hairy flaps, or dewlaps, that hang from their throat. Called bells, these flaps may help with mating rituals or heat regulation.

FEATURED FAMILY

Give It a Try

It's a beautiful, sunny July day. The temperature is 59 °F (15 °C). The twins chase each other and jump over fallen trees as they follow their mother to a quiet pond. The mother walks into the water, dips her muzzle, and grabs pond weed. The firstborn twin stops playing with her sister. She walks into the water, dips her muzzle, and grasps some pond weed. Her sister, still playing on shore, runs into the water and bumps into her twin, making them both fall into the shallow water.

Usually anti-social, moose will "**yard-up**" in small groups in winter.

6 YEARS

▸ Trophy sized antlers grown on a bull moose

▸ Start of prime reproductive age for both male and female

CLOSE-UP
Antlers

Mature males grow antlers up to five feet wide, using them for defense and to compete during mating. They shed them after breeding.

CHAPTER THREE
LIFE LESSONS

The moose calf survived predators, weather, disease, and humans for a year. Just as the mother is about to give birth in the late spring again, she chases off her offspring. She is forceful, making sure the yearling is far from where she has chosen to give birth. Fortunately, it stopped nursing months ago when it learned to eat plants and twigs.

Moose may migrate seasonally to give birth, **rut**, and winter. They can travel a few miles to more than 60 miles (96.6 km). Although they tend to roam their habitat alone, moose may "yard up" in small groups during the winter when the snow is deep, and they need to keep walkways clear to food. Moose lose up to 20 percent of their body weight during winter because they eat twigs, shrubs, and bark.

Fall is rut, or breeding, season. The bulls start to **bellow**. This loud call attracts the females. Males also splash their antlers or bell with urine to lure the females. Because the males usually spend the year apart from each

(10) YEARS

- Largest antlers grown on a bull

other, they come together during the mating season and battle each other with their huge antlers. They fight to prove their mating dominance. Most battles are minor. On occasion, the fight is bad enough that a moose dies from its injuries, and the winner mates with the cows. Males and females ignore each other before and after mating season.

A cow is pregnant for about 8 months. Depending on the cow's age and health, she will have one, two, or three calves. The healthier and older a cow, the greater the chance she has of having twins or triplets, although triplets are rare.

FEATURED FAMILY

This is How It's Done

After the family of three have strolled from shrubs to dogwood, they find willow by a creek. The leaves are turning yellow and orange in the cooling temperatures and shorter days. The twins reach up to grab the leaves that haven't yet fallen to the ground. They still can't reach as high as their mother, but they've put on weight and grew taller with all the lush vegetation they ate over the summer. A willow ptarmigan lands nearby, blending in with leaves as the family chews its cud.

CLOSE-UP
Velvet

Velvet is the skin that covers the antlers. Velvet is filled with blood vessels to provide nutrients for the antlers' rapid growth. In late summer, the males scrape off the velvet, right before they start to mate.

(12) YEARS

▸ Typical end of life in wild

LIFE LESSONS

Moose rarely live to be 16 years old. Opposite other wild animals, the lifespan of a moose in captivity decreases by years.

Moose are not on the International Union for Conservation of Nature and Natural Resources (IUCN) Red List of Threatened Species. In fact, they are listed as "Least Concern." However, biologists become concerned when moose populations in their areas of the world drop.

CLOSE-UP
Skin

Male moose have a special thick skin that covers their front and their neck. This extra protection, almost like a shield, is needed for mating season when the males fight and wound each other for a female's attention.

──────────── FEATURED FAMILY ────────────

Practice Makes Perfect

After protecting them and helping them find food all winter, the twins' mother forces them to leave her. The young moose bed down in a birch forest and are able to find succulent green leaves on the nearby trees. The twins stand close to each other as they chew their cud. After they swallow, they move to the next bite of leaves. Mid-day, they walk to a pond and enter the cold water, ignoring a beaver's tail warning. They both dive under and rip salty pond weed from the muddy bottom.

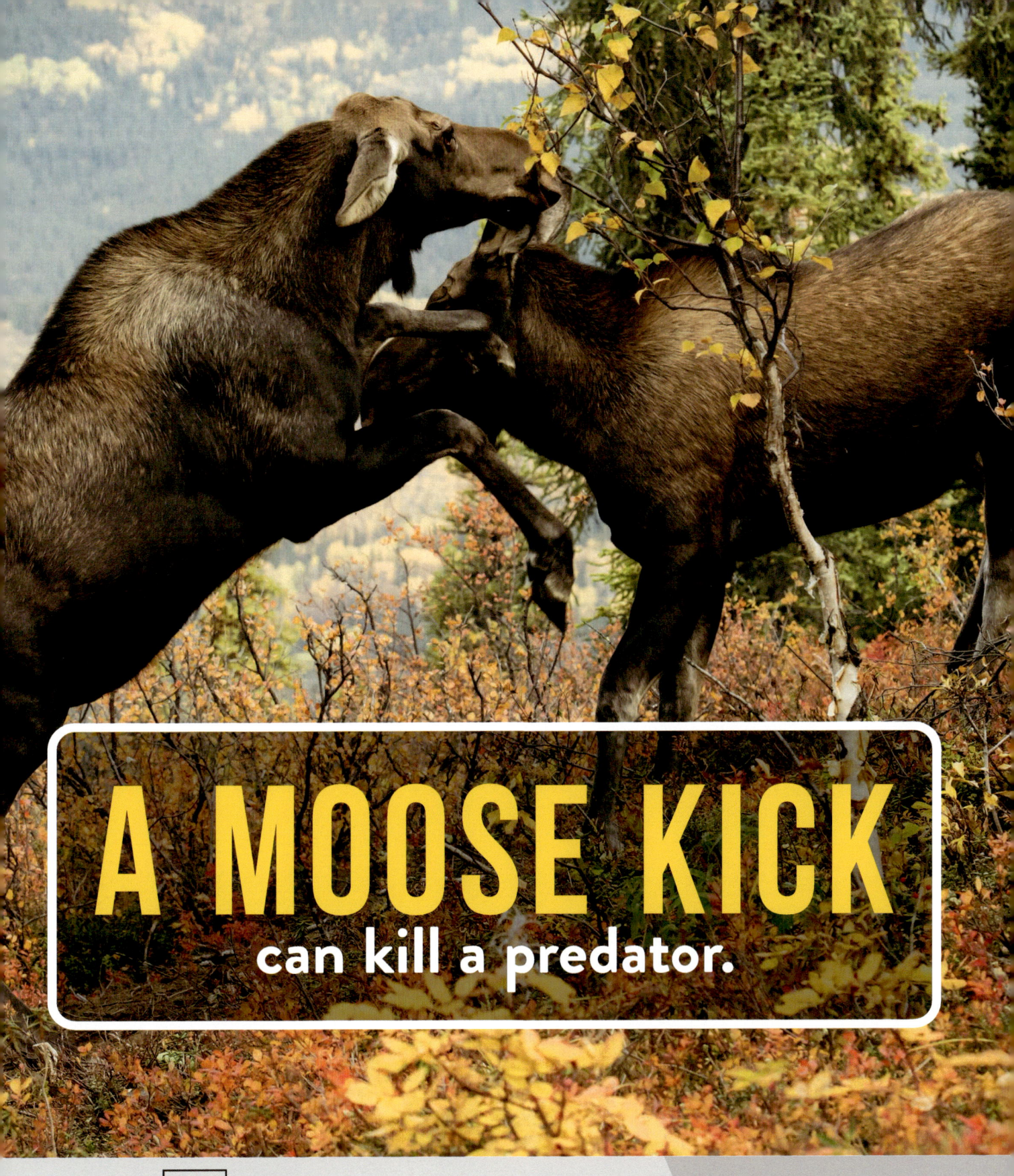

A MOOSE KICK
can kill a predator.

15 - 20 YEARS
▸ Maximum lifespan

LIFE LESSONS

CHAPTER FOUR
HELPING MOOSE SURVIVE

Moose face various threats, including habitat destruction and collisions with vehicles. However, climate change has introduced additional challenges that can threaten their survival. Overheating becomes a major issue. The thick fur which offers protection in colder climates becomes a liability as temperatures rise. This creates heat stress. This condition increases their heart rate and forces them to seek shade or cool water, often at the expense of eating. As a result, moose may struggle to gain the necessary weight during the summer months, leaving them without sufficient fat reserves to endure harsh winter conditions.

Warmer winters also mean that deer enter moose territory. Deer poop contains a **parasitic** brainworm. The moose may swallow poop and the brainworm while eating nearby plants. The larvae travel to the moose's brain and spinal cord, causing nerve damage. Brainworms rarely affect deer, but will eventually kill the moose.

Warm winters can also create an overabundance of ticks. Biologists have been shocked to discover moose covered with as many as 90,000 ticks. These ticks drain about 24 gallons (90.8 liters) of blood from a single moose. This loss of blood weakens the moose and can lead to death. Large tick populations also create problems for pregnant moose, as many are unable to carry their calves to term.

Besides tackling global warming, researchers believe they have solutions. One is to have planned hunts to reduce the number of animal hosts for the ticks. Another solution is using a **fungal spore** in soil which which attaches to the tick and produces chemicals to kill it.

In the past decade, officials at the Minnesota Department of Natural Resources (DNR) realized the moose population was declining. Hunters were not permitted to kill the animal in 2013. That same year, the DNR launched a research project to better understand why moose **mortality** and how to improve their chances of survival. They used GPS collars to track the animals and collect data. Early findings showed that climate change and health problems were the main reasons for the population decline. This research, the largest and most advanced project of its kind in North America at the time, could also help other states and countries with their efforts to conserve moose.

Right now, the moose's existence is not threatened. With careful conservation, the majestic moose will never be a vulnerable or endangered species.

FAMILY ALBUM
SNAPSHOTS

Four-chambered stomachs allow moose to eat a lot of food and store more than 100 pounds of it.

People in Europe call moose elk, while in the United States, there are the moose species and elk species.

A common nickname for moose is "rubber-nosed swamp donkeys." This name is probably because of their huge, floppy ears and hulking faces.

Despite their gigantic size, moose are excellent swimmers. They can swim 10 miles (16.1 km) without stopping.

The moose is a huge animal—snout, antlers, and body. But it has a tail that is only 3 inches (7.6 cm) long!

Moose do not have any top front teeth. They use their upper lip to grip their food. Moose have 32 teeth total—12 on top and 20 on bottom.

As bulls prepare for the rut, they don't eat anything for 2 weeks. These male moose can lose about 20 percent of their body weight.

The heaviest recorded moose was in Kenai Penisula in Alaska weighing in at 1,697 pounds (769.7 kg) with antlers. The heaviest recorded antlers were 75 pounds (34 kg)!

Before bedding down at night, a moose will travel upwind first. Then it swings back in a partial circle.

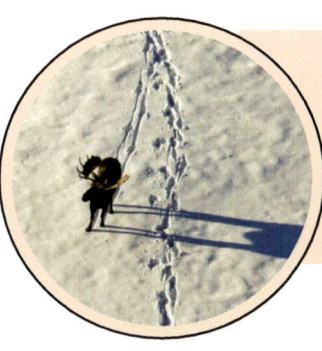

Alaskan moose have lived where the coldest temperature was recorded in Alaska. In 1971, the temperature was -80° F (-62° C) along the Dalton Highway near the Gates of the Arctic National Park and Preserve.

SNAPSHOTS 29

WORDS to Know

aquatic — taking place in or around water

bellow — a deep hollow sound

deciduous — falling off at a certain stage

fungal — spore a reproductive body of one cell that lives on dead matter

mortality — death

muzzle — an animal's nose and jaw

parasitic — relating to an organism that needs a host to live

regurgitate — to be thrown back or out again

rut — the period of breeding season

tines — slender, pointed parts

LEARN MORE

Books

Castaldo, Nancy. *The Wolves and Moose of Isle Royale: Restoring an Island Ecosystem.* New York: Clarion Books, 2022.

Gish, Melissa. *Moose.* Mankato, Minn.: Creative Education and Creative Paperbacks, 2023.

Hubbard, Ben. *Wolves vs. Moose: Food Chain Fights.* Minneapolis: Lerner Publications Company, 2024.

Websites

"Moose." National Geographic Kids.

https://kids.nationalgeographic.com/animals/mammals/facts/moose

"Moose (Alces alces)." Alaska Department of Fish and Game.

https://www.adfg.alaska.gov/index.cfm?adfg!moose.main

"Moose: Did You Know?" National Park Service.

https://www.nps.gov/articles/moose-did-you-know.htm

Documentaries

Moose Attack. New York: Pangolin Pictures, 2010.

"Moose: Life of a Twig Eater." PBS Nature (Season 34, Episode 10). New York: The WNET Group, 2016.

Alaskan Moose: A Journey with Giants. Tucson: Open Lens Productions, 2010.

Note: Every effort has been made to ensure that any websites listed above were active at the time of publication. However, because of the nature of the Internet, it is impossible to guarantee that these sites will remain active indefinitely or that their contents will not be altered.

Visit

CHEYENNE MOUNTAIN ZOO

One of the eight institutions to house moose and the only U.S. zoo in the mountains, visitors can see Atka, an orphaned Alaskan moose.
4250 Cheyenne Mountain Zoo Road
Colorado Springs, CO 80906

ISLE ROYALE NATIONAL PARK, MICHIGAN

Without predators on this island in Lake Superior that you get to by ferry, seaplane, or private boat, you'll observe moose behaviors not often seen other places.
800 East Lakeshore Drive
Houghton, MI 49931

GRAND TETON NATIONAL PARK

May through September is the perfect time to catch moose at a lake's edge or river's edge or at the mouth of the Cascade Canyon in this park.
P.O. Box 170
Moose, WY 83012

MINNESOTA ZOO

Moose have made their home here since 1978.
13000 Zoo Boulevard
Apple Valley, MN 55124

INDEX

Alaska, 5, 7, 8, 29
antlers, 7, 13, 17, 18, 19, 20, 21, 28
behavior, 9, 20
climate Change, 25, 26
conservation, 22, 26
Denali, 5
diet 13, 14, 15
ecosystems, 5
habitat, 13, 19, 25

heat Stress, 25
mating, 13, 16, 18, 20, 21, 22
migration, 19
national Park, 5, 29
offspring, 5, 8, 9, 13, 15, 19
parasites, 25
population Decline, 26
predators, 8, 9, 19
survival, 25, 26